GOD WORKS THROUGH SILENCE

The Creative Silence And God's Workshop

By:
Robert A. Russell

Copyright © 2019 by Audio Enlightenment Press All rights reserved. No part of this publication may be reproduced, distributed, or transmitted in any form or by any means, including photocopying, recording, or other electronic or mechanical methods, without the prior written permission of the publisher, except in the case of brief quotations embodied in critical reviews and certain other noncommercial uses permitted by copyright law. All our editions are textually watermarked to prevent copyright violation.

Printed in the United States of America

First Printing, 2019

ISBN 978-941489-62-8

www.RobertARussell.Org

Introduction

More than twenty years ago, The Creative Silence and God's Workshop were issued in paperback edition. They have always been among the most popular of our books. In this edition, the best of the two books has been retained and much of my thinking of the past twenty years has been incorporated. No one in the process of growth could sanction the reprinting of a volume exactly as it was written years before.

It is my hope that this book will meet the needs of those who have grown with me in spiritual understanding, in awareness of the height and depth of God's love, and in realization of man's Oneness with Him; and that those who are taking their first steps on this joyous journey will find through it the Wisdom whose ways are ways of pleasantness and all whose paths are peace.

Robert A. Russell

Table of Contents

Introduction iii

Part One The Creative Silence 1

   Chapter 1 Know Thyself 1

   Chapter 2 Understanding the Silence 13

   Chapter 3 Principles of The Silence 25

   Chapter 4 The Principle of Universal Mind 33

   Chapter 5 The One Mind Active Through Man 41

Part Two God's Workshop The Mechanics of Silence .. 49

   Chapter 1 Relaxation 49

   Chapter 2 Concentration 53

   Chapter 3 Meditation 59

   Chapter 4 Visualization 63

   Chapter 5 Realization 69

   Chapter 6 How to Give A Treatment in The Silence .. 73

Appendix Suggested Exercises to Produce Relaxation ... 81

Part One
The Creative Silence

Chapter 1
Know Thyself

When the Delphian Oracle was asked by a seeker of knowledge what was the open sesame of all knowledge and all wisdom, the brief answer was "Know thyself." Wisely spoken, for to know one's self is the source of all health, supply, knowledge, power and happiness.

All life from the smallest atom to the largest planet is animated from the center outward. If you know the nature of a drop of water, you know the nature of the ocean. If you understand a lump of gold, you know the nature of all gold. If you understand a piece of clay, you know the nature of all clay—whether it is a clay house or a clay elephant. If you know the structure of an atom, you know the physical structure of man. If you know your own Soul and your own mind and your own Spirit, you know God, for they are a part of Him.

God created man in his own image. This image is not that of the physical body, for God is Spirit. It is our spirituality that is a counterpart of God. No one has ever seen the real man. The body of flesh apparent to the senses is merely the clothing of the soul.

In the eternal search for truth, two types of thought are engaged—the objective. One seeks among the externals and asks why. Science and religion are searching for Truth from the opposite ends of the same pole. They are closer and closer together all the time and ultimately will meet. When they do, it will revolutionize the entire field of science and religion. Truth cannot be changed or injured by either science or religion. It will always prove itself.

How are we to know the man within? By self-analysis and contemplation. We must learn to enter the inner sanctuary of our souls, shut out the world of senses, and turn our thoughts to the God within the Silence. By getting acquainted with the possibilities and powers of our souls, we know the Divine. By knowing the fragment, we know the Whole.

Behold I bring you glad tidings of great joy, which shall be to all men. It is possible to get immediate answers to prayers, immediate results from the application of Truth, and immediate recognition from God. Spirit is Infinite Responsiveness, everywhere and evenly present. God is no respecter of persons and the law of His response applies equally to all persons everywhere.

It does not matter how many mistakes you have made, how many times you have failed, or what you have believed. The moment you enter the Secret Place of the Most High, conditions will begin to change and your affairs will improve. In the Silence, God can reach you. In the Silence, you can reach God. In the twinkling of the eye, without delay, you can enter the Divine Presence.

Through the silent activity of your thought, God acts through you and with you. You are augmented by all the good which the Universe contains. The light always shines, but you must open your spiritual eyes before the darkness disappears. There is no punishment for having been in the darkness, but there is great joy in the outer. God is Spirit, and it is as Spirit that He sees you in secret, that is, as you know yourself in your spiritual nature. He rewards you openly. As you turn toward the Light, the Light turns toward you.

By allowing God to take possession of you, you reach out to Him. By withdrawing your conscious thought from the relative world and centering it in the One, you open the channel through which your needs are supplied, your desire granted.

To control condition through the power of correct thinking, you must seek to realize the presence of the desired result before it is visible to the physical eye. By forming the mental equivalent, you form the spiritual prototype. The spiritual prototype, being the origin of the thing, is the cause of it; it is not bound nor limited by any existent fact. It is able to transcend the fact as it appears and produce results in accord with the belief you have given to it. As water reaches its own level by its own weight, so consciousness externalizes at the level of its own conception. It is done unto us not as we hope or wish but as we really believe deep down in the wellspring of our being.

No matter how persistent the disease, how intricate the problem or how devastating the lack, the moment you enter the Silence and find within yourself the equivalent of your desires, conditions will begin to improve and your spiritual claim will be met. The Law is Infinite. But it can give to you only what you can take and you can take only what you really are.

With God all thing are possible. His universe is fundamentally good. To be One with God is to be in the Kingdom of Heaven.

All work in the silence is for the purpose of unfolding the Divine Nature through man, of making him more conscious of himself and consequently more at One with God, of enlarging his concept of God.

Who is God? What is God?

God is Infinite Life. God is Infinite Mind. God is Infinite Spirit. God is Infinite Truth. God is Infinite Love.
God is Infinite Intelligence.
God is Universal Consciousness. God is Cause.
God is Creator and Creation.
God is Omnipotence, Omniscience, Omnipresence. God is Absolute Law.
God is Positive Principle.
God is Power, Force, Energy. God is I AM, the Eternal.

Mind is one of the many words which we use in the effort to clarify our understanding of the universal creative and sustaining power which we call God. It is synonymous with Spirit, Life, Wisdom, Intelligence, Principle, Law. We enlarge our comprehension of a particular phase or attribute of God by concentrated study of, or meditation upon, a term; and by raising the level of our consciousness, we increase our receptivity or capacity to make use of this Universal Power on our own individual plane.

The mind of man works both objectively and subjectively. The objective mind interprets the world of the senses; signs, sounds, heat and cold. The subjective mind is not so obvious but is none the less capable of proof. Under hypnosis the subjective mind of the patient is active, the objective mind being temporarily incapable of response. The subjective mind receives commands and acts upon them, the entire body being affected by the will of the hypnotist. We have other phenomena in our daily lives which are not so spectacular although no less remarkable. Our ability to remember—in fact our lack of ability to forget, habits and dreams depend upon the subconscious mind.

If then we accept these two phases or aspects of individual mind, we must conclude that they are counterparts of the Universal Mind; our minds in their two phases are our shares of the Universal Mind.

The Universal Mind is the creator. It is the First Cause. Being universal, It cannot act upon the plane of the individual and particular except through the forms which It creates. All creational form is a manifestation of the Mind of God. All nature is the objectifying of the ideas of Spirit; plant and animal instincts are evidences of this Mind. Mind is the force in matter that results in the concrete living forms which make up our visible world. Attributes of this Mind are expressed by the adjectives, Omnipotent, Omniscient, Omnipresent, Omniactive. It acts through the Law; It is impersonal. It responds through the subjective mind of man on just the level of his consciousness.

When man makes his choice through his objective mind and calls upon Universal Mind through his individual subjective mind, he releases Infinite Power which has only one purpose—to carry out the task given to It. It is the Creator and the thing created. Man is the perfect idea of this Mind. Its only limitation is found in man himself, for the response of Mind can be on no higher level than that to which he has attained.

The individual objective mind in man is a distinguishing and identifying factor; through it, his world is given meaning, for it interprets the testimony of the sense. Man can take his testimony or evidence, study it, discover relationships, analyze their effect, draw conclusions, make decision, and alter his conduct accordingly. He has will-power, the power of choice, the power of reason. Reason is the highest power given to him; through it he can choose his line of conduct and direct his life. The objective mind reasons both inductively and deductively. It responds to education; it can be made orderly and can be taught to recognize the right from the wrong. It is the governing power of the subjective mind. Consciously or unconsciously, it is giving commands which the willing servant carries out. The responsibility for the results as manifested in living conditions, human relationships and financial success rests upon the relationship between man's objective and subjective mind.

The individual subjective mind is the bridge between Universal Mind and the individual objective mind. It relates the individual to the Creative Mind of God. It is here that the Holy Spirit does His work. It has no purpose apart from that of the objective mind; it has no discrimination in accepting or rejecting or evaluating the impressions made upon it. It exists to bring about the desires of the objective mind. It is the creative power of the individual. It takes whatever information is giving it and acts upon it. The only reasoning of which it is capable is deductive. It is the body-builder, renewing tissues and cells and controlling the so-called involuntary processes, such as the action of the heart, lungs, and digestive organs.

It is the seat of the emotions and intuitions. While it acts on suggestion, it is highly creative. It takes our spoken or unspoken thoughts and feelings and suggestions and builds them into concrete and tangible things such as health, favorable environment, improved financial condition, better personal relationship. The higher we raise our power to make use of the individual subjective mind, the closer we are to God. By increasing our awareness, we can rise to undreamed of heights, for there are no limitations of time or space in Mind. Since the subjective mind acts without hindrance from any source except the objective mind which sets it in motion, it must be freed from any suggestion of evil or fear.

In the Silence, we bring the objective mind to a pause and work in the subjective mind in which we are Universal. All healing and all demonstrations are made in the Universal Mind, the Creative Mind of Spirit. In the Universal Mind, a new order of being manifests—a being who is One with the Source of all knowledge and all supply.

In the Silence, we manifest in our consciousness the Spirit of God. Through our positive and constructive thinking, the individual mind becomes one with the Absolute Universal Mind, making perfect realization possible. As we turn away from the world of the senses, we enter the Within, the Source of all things.

God is unity; man is diversity. United, they manifest harmony, the true expression of the Silence. The soul is the constant expression of the I AM. It is the same whether Universal or individual. Heaven and harmony mean the same thing; when we work and think in harmony, all our action is constructive.

The Silence is subjective; It is never negative, passive or inactive. Those who enter the inner chamber to think of nothing or just to be still will be disappointed in the results. The Silence is far more than just being quiet; It is far more than meditation upon the undifferentiated. It is thinking in the most vital and dynamic way that the mind can think. It is thinking with God, developing a capacity to comprehend the wisdom and power of Divine Mind.

To practice the Silence is to train the mind to open itself to the greater harmonies, to become more and more aware of the Power and Substance that make all things possible.

The Silence touches both the inside and outside of all things. It is positive and dynamic; It comprehends the full ear within the kernel of corn, the lily within the bulb, the mighty oak within the acorn, the chick within the shell, the man within the germ, the form within the idea. Life proceeds from a common center and through the Creative Mind manifests as form.

Prayer and answer are the very same thing. The answer is in the prayer. Praying is the process of setting an idea in motion on the subjective side of Life. The prayer will be answered according to the belief of the one who prays. Everyone that asketh receiveth. But if you pray for one thing and believe in something else, the answer will be in accord with your belief. You cannot fool Principle, but you can fool yourself. When your belief is equal to your prayer, you are equal to your need.

Spiritual self-mastery surmounts every obstacle, dissipates every obstruction, heals every disease. It is greater than any condition when we know that we are dealing with Principle and not with personality, that Mind is the only actor and that nothing moves except as Mind moves it.

The consistent, positive, aggressive mental attitude toward the Truth, which is the opposite thought of any negative condition into visibility. Every positive thought is a step in the processional march toward the goal, the realization that in him we live and move and have our being.

Prayer is a mental act. When we pray, we are dealing with Mind, the Cause of everything that is, was or ever shall be. Mind molds substance into form. People money, animals, flowers, food, skyscrapers, trains, aeroplanes—all are the products of Mind. Because Mind works with the Substance from which all things are made, our prayer has power to create what we pray for.

Where does life find you today? Is your present position to your liking? The answer ought to be affirmative. Whether it is or not, the Law says you are just where you belong. If you didn't belong where you are, you wouldn't be there. Every man, like Judas, goes to his own place, that is, goes where his mind takes him. Nothing can get you out of that place but yourself. Others may help you by pointing the way, but extrication can come at last only through your own consciousness.

Your position in life is always determined by your habitual thought of yourself, that is, by what you give Mind to work with. Men will know you and accept you by what you persistently know about yourself—by what Mind knows about you. If you think well of yourself, others will think the same thing of you. If you think you are a worm of the dust, others will want to step on you. As you hold yourself in Mind, so you will be held. It is not conceit to think well of yourself, for the Self referred to is the Inner Man which is God. All the qualities and attributes of Spirit are you insofar as you make use of them.

Ancient mystics used to instruct their pupils to cross their hands over their chest many times a day and say in an audible voice the words, "Wonderful, wonderful, wonderful me," while feeling the Presence of God. We would do well to follow their example.

When you think of Yourself as the potential cause of everything that is; when you see and know that Self as the act and actor, the cause and effect, the idea and manifestation, the Alpha and Omega; when you see the inside and the outside as the same thing, and see them as one complete whole; when you see the idea and object as one and your word as an accomplished fact, you will demonstrate the Truth.

There is only one Mind in the Universe to think with, and that Mind is your Mind. It knows everything and is everything. It is never confused and never divided. It controls objective expressions through subjective recognition. It will produce for you whatever you believe It to be. The law of manifestation is absolute. Action and reaction are always equal to each other. What you know about yourself in this Mind, It knows about you.

In any condition, there is no one and nothing to treat but yourself. Every prayer will reach its own level. When you know yourself as the answer to your prayer because there is only one Activity, you will be invincible as the Cause of all your Good. The possibilities of your prayer are limited only by your mental equivalents and concepts.

Seek ye first the kingdom of God and his righteousness and all these things shall be added unto you. Seek first the knowledge of the Christ in you — the Heaven in you — the Power in you — the God in you.

The ultimate goal of the Silence is a complete emancipation from all discord of every nature. The place to start from is your own mind. This is the only Mind there is, the only God there is, the only Power there is, and the only Heaven there is. Realize that God and you are the very same Being. I and the Father are one. This is the Truth which Jesus taught. Only as you enter the Divine Self can you become the conscious master of you supply, health, harmony and happiness.

Henceforth, know yourself as a Spiritual Being. Know your body as a Divine idea. Do not crystallize yourself in a limited sphere of consciousness. The Real Body, Jesus pointed out, is Spiritual. It will serve you to the degree that you realize its Presence.

Jesus as a skyscraper is built by many separate bricks. Just as one becomes a musician through many separate lessons, you will crucify, or do away with, the limited ideas of yourself and God through many separate experiences in the Silence. In it you will learn to think better of yourself than you ever have before.

A diseased body not vibrating in unison with the great throb of the Universe can be healed by restoring that equilibrium. The great throb of the Universe is Divine Mind whose vibration is the Universal Law. By getting into perfect rhythm or harmony with that Mind, man can restore health and power to his body.

Establishing yourself in the movement of Divine Mind result in the restoration of your Spiritual Self. If your demonstration are not quickly and easily made, if your prayers are not answered, you can be certain that the finite self is in the way. So long as there is any imposition of this self upon God, there can be no quickening of the consciousness toward Universal Supply.

In the Silence, you step out of yourself and into God. You reach the fullness of God, your unity with the Whole, through the realization that I AM alone speaks, thinks and acts .The more spiritual your growth, the greater your capability for perceiving the things of the spirit. The loftier your spiritual enlightenment, the finer and higher your perception until you come to realize, know and comprehend the ever-hovering Presence. Through enlarging your consciousness, you will learn that the angel of the Lord encampeth about.

The acme philosophy is the knowledge of yourself, the Within. That everything real, permanent, God-like and eternal is incorporated in you is the most vital knowledge the Universe demand of you. You find this Truth in the Silence.

Chapter 2
Understanding the Silence

The religions of the world that have meant most to man's spiritual development have taught and practiced the mental and physical discipline which we call the Silence. All have pointed to one Central Life and Intelligence from which all creatures draw their livingness and without which nothing could exist. The Christian religion has made the strongest appeal to the thinking races of the world because it has given the greatest value to individual life. Jesus taught that man is an individualized center of God-Conscious Life, a Soul through which God expresses Himself as individuality, and that the significance of His incarnation in the flesh is the promotion of man's individuality to the point at which he accepts his own divinity. Because the Christian religion is self-evident, demonstrable, provable, practical and true, it has stood the test of reason and time.

The universe in which we live is a universe of Law and Spirit which are complementary to each other. We have discovered that we reap what we have sown and that we stand or fall according to the tendency of our thought.

We become like that which we think upon. As a man thinketh in his heart, so is he, God manifests Himself in us according to the habitual tendency of our thought. Each individual contacts the Universal Divine Mind through his own mentality. It differentiates and personifies Itself in us according to the character of our thinking.

What we contemplate, we become. If we contemplate beauty, we become beautiful. If we contemplate love, we become lovable. To the degree that we contemplate an idea, to that degree its particular quality is born in us. As an individual, man can become receptive to any idea or though he selects. To the degree that he can embody that idea to the exclusion of all other, to that degree he becomes the absolute manifestation of it. The essence and quality of Divine Reality flow through any individual who makes himself receptive to It, for the Inner Self and the outer self are one.

Since everything wait upon your thought, you must become receptive to the Divine Self which acts in you to the degree that you accept It. There is nothing too great or too small for this Self to do. But God can come in the fullness of His Unity only as you provide the channel for His coming. It makes no difference what you may be seeking—guidance, healing, money, peace, joy, happiness, the Spirit can give you only what you can take. The measure of your taking is determined by the degree of your receptivity. God interprets Himself to you through your own mind.

Faith in God is the channel through which God moves. But just as water will not flow through a hose that is kinked, so the Spirit cannot flow through you and into your experience until the channel is cleared. To be receptive you must empty yourself of all personal willing and thinking. You must set aside old preconceived opinion, prejudices and fears, and withdraw from every activity of the personal man.

Blessed are the poor in spirit for theirs is the kingdom of heaven. The individual, poor in spirit, is the humble—he who knows I can of mine own self do nothing…The Father that dwelleth in me, he doeth the works. He is detached from the material environment.

So long as we are attached to anything, we are not free; we linger on a lower level. Our detachment must be a complete thing. We must be spectators. We must empty ourselves that we may be filled. Following the example of Jesus, we must prepare ourselves for the flow of Life and Truth into our minds, bodies and affairs. If we would receive abundantly, we must create a capacity for abundance. We must be absolutely empty, and this state is what we try to bring about in the Silence.

The object of the Silence is to bring the individual into direct contact with the Infinite Mind, the Cause and Ultimate of all that is. Through the practice of inaction, the realization comes that the act and the actor, the cause and the effect are one and the same.

The simplest explanation of the Silence is the statement of Jesus: Ye shall know the truth, and the truth shall make you free. The ultimate purpose is to bring about true purity of thought, singleness of vision, and the substitution of the spiritual for the material viewpoint.

The practice of the Silence antedates Christianity by hundreds of years. The early Hebrews thought of God as dwelling in the Silence. Elisha found that He was not in the windstorms, the fire or the earthquake, but in the stillness. Plato some 2300 years ago not only discerned the value of the Silence and practiced it himself but made it an integral and important part of his work and teaching, as did Socrates and many others.

The Silence is what the word implies—a place of stillness. It does not have a specific location, dimension or boundary, nor can it be measured or compassed. Metaphysically speaking, it is a state of mind, the simplest function of consciousness. Theologically speaking, it is a form of prayer, the most subtle form known.

Belonging to and encompassing the intangible world of Spirit, It is beyond the range of sense. It becomes real only to those who in a state of mental and physical abstraction withdraw from the illusions of the material world to become the instruments or channels for Spirit. It is an unconfined state in which all labor is effortless. Its activities are governed by the Laws of Receptivity and Correspondence. We draw from the Universal Subjective Mind what we bring to it.

The devotee of the Silence listens to Himself. He prays to Himself and looks within his own Mind for the answers to his prayers, the solution of his problems. The Infinite Thinker, who knows and gives all things, comes bearing the gifts sought. If the listener needs guidance, he calls for it saying, "I now let Infinite Intelligence within me acquaint my mind and tell me what to do," The Infinite Knower, obedient to the Law of Receptivity which demands a conscious mental acceptance, will respond to him.

In the Silence there is peace for the peaceful. There is health for the healthful. There is prosperity for the prosperous. There is harmony for the harmonious. There are riches for the rich. There is happiness for the happy. There is no lack of any of these things in Divine Mind, but we can only express that which we consciously accept. Nothing can be wholly ours until we accept ourselves as that which is the object of our desire.

All the good things of life respond to us as we respond to them, but we must surrender everything that is unlike that which we call good. The world in which we live is peopled with ideas and thoughts, each one of which is matched, or has its correlative, on the invisible side of life. All things exist as possibilities in Divine Mind; otherwise we could not even think of them. But our faith and mental acceptance determine when and how fully they shall come to us. Every idea is matched by Reality; that is, it exists potentially.

The Impersonal God gives to all alike. Son thou art ever with me, and all that I have is thine. There is nothing we can want that He does not want for us. We can press any claim and know that it will be met. It is for us to decide what that claim shall be. Since we are individualized centers of God and can never be separated from Principle, God is always on our side, and nothing is impossible to Him.

In this practice, we make common property of the teachings of Jesus Christ. We penetrate the One Presence which has never been violated and which knows no lack. There is something within us all which longs for this glorious experience in the still and silent Presence. The heart pants after the Higher Self and the soul of man will never be satisfied until he finds It.

In the Silence, we are practicing one of the most vital aspects of prayer. Be still and know that I am God... The Lord is in his holy temple; let all the earth keep silent before him.... When thou prayest, enter into thy closet, and when thou hast shut thy door, pray to thy Father which is in secret; and thy Father which seeth in secret shall reward thee openly.

The closet refers to the subjective mind, the creative medium in man. It is through the subjective mind that God acts through us.

The Psalmist speaks of the subjective mind as the city of God and of its activity as a river. There is a river, the streams whereof shall make glad the city of God, the holy place of the tabernacle of the most High. A river is symbolical of purpose, of fluidic thought, of a medium of commerce; the city is symbolical of a center of activity and distribution. A river is not a stationary thing like an ocean or a lake; it is in a constant state of flow. It gives life and fertility to the country through which it flows; it has a certain destination. The water that it carries is representative of the vital energy which means life to the earth. A man's consciousness is in truth the City of God. The purpose of the river is to purify, cleanse and establish that which it touches. God is in the midst of her; she shall not be moved; God shall help her, and that right early. Her refers to the feminine or subjective mind.

The subjective mind which controls all the vital processes of the body is involuntary in its action but through conscious direction in the Silence, it can be stimulated and directed. Be ye transformed by the renewing of the mind. You can regenerate your body by controlling your subjective mind.

The Soul transcends the body and forever remains the same. It never violates its own nature or integrity. It will never be more nor less than it already is. The Soul is God manifesting through our individual consciousness.

Webster defines soul as spirit; essence, life; animating principle or part. The body is an effect or manifestation of the Soul. The body can never die because it was never alive. When the body is no longer a fit instrument for the Soul, it is dropped by the wayside and the Soul clothes itself with another body of more perfect form. What does this prove? Only that you, the Consciousness, are the Real Self, for in the experience called death, Consciousness and

Life leave the body at the same time. The Soul is an individualized center of God-Conscious life.

Jesus said, I and my Father are one. The Father in me and I in him. The great point of controversy between Jesus and the Jews was that Thou, being a man, makest thyself God. Like many today, they failed to understand the Real Man upon whom the whole Christian philosophy is based. Actually the term man refers to material form or physical body which is an idea of Mind, an effect. Jesus is the name of the son of the human carpenter of Nazareth, but he never identified Himself (the Christ in him) with the personal Jesus or his body. He knew His Power, Life and Consciousness to be Mind or Soul.

The belief in a material or separate selfhood has been the cause of all our inferiority, helplessness and limitation. St. John the Divine seemed to understand this error in our thinking when he voiced the words: Beloved, now are we the sons of God, and it doth not yet appear what we shall be; but we know that when he shall appear, we shall be like him, for we shall see him as he is. As long as we think of ourselves as mortal, we lack dominion. When we are able to distinguish between the material and the Spiritual man and can hold the Christ concept, we shall discover that we are identical with God. St. John used the word like, meaning in quality or degree.

Since you are life and Life is God, only God can live. Since God is Mind, and you are the manifestation of Mind, only Mind can think. Only Mind can see. Only Mind can hear. Only Mind can speak. Mind, the Principle of Life, never enters or becomes attached to the body any more than you, peering into a mirror, enter the mirror. You will gain dominion over the earth (your body and affairs) to the degree that you are able to grasp this concept and hold it in consciousness. Jesus had no life but the Life of God; you have no life but the Life of God. The thoughts you think not only affect yourself but extend outward and affect others, for there is only the One Mind.

We must accept our mental and spiritual heritage. We are individual expressions of God, Spirit made manifest, the form selected to bear witness to the Truth. The extent to which we can draw upon Intelligence and Power depends upon our self-development. We have the latent capacity to become anything we wish. We receive sense impressions from the world about us; we interpret these and they become meaningful to us; we base our conduct on the result of our reasoning about them; we have the power to choose the line of our action. More than this, we have within us creative power which will bring to pass the thing which we choose and on which our hearts are set. Our responsibility for choosing aright is tremendous, for all we have to do to make heaven or hell here on earth, to bring about success or failure here and now is to think. We can think ourselves up or down.

Until we function consciously in and from the Soul, until we act from the Self in which all power resides, we shall be unable to control our forces.

The masterful individuality which speaks from the soul is the Supreme Self, or I AM of God. This I AM is always conscious of Itself. It responds to the man outside as he responds to It. Spirit knows man only at the level of his ability to know himself.

Through the spirit (I AM), we can in the Silence establish a means of communion between the man outside and the Man Inside. Each one of us must contact God through his own mind until He takes possession of our consciousness.

The secret of spiritual power is the individual consciousness of union with God. The I AM is Good. It is Love, Life, Law Intelligence and Power, but it interprets Itself to man only as he mentally embodies the whole, only as he recognizes the I AM as the changeless Principle of his own mind. The more completely he becomes conscious of this union, the more power and dominion he expresses. Health, harmony, happiness and prosperity are effects, not causes.

When we act from the standpoint of body or personality, we separate life from living, Spirit from matter. We cannot hope to claim our Good, for we are reversing the process. If God is all, there cannot be God and something else. There can be no shadows without light. There can be no outside without an inside. There can be no Jesus without a Christ. There can be no effect without a cause. It is done unto you as you believe. We limit the expression of the I AM through our belief in limitation. The Divine Law will produce anything we choose. It will produce prosperity instead of poverty, health instead of sickness.

The Law is, but It must be definitely specialized. Until we specialize It, It is only a latent possibility. Through this Law, we set the Principle in which we live in motion. When we do not use the Law consciously and constructively, we are using It unconsciously and, it may be, destructively.

Prayer is the mental act through which we specialize the Law for specific purposes. In the Silence, we are responsive to the Law. Silence is the home of the soul. It is always at rest, always at peace, always in repose.

The unseen and silent forces in the universe are the strongest. Physical activity is noisy and slow; Infinite activity is silent and quick. We hear nothing as gravity holds our material world together. There is no sound as the sun each day lifts billions of tons of water from the earth. Neither is there any perceptible friction or noise in the operation of electricity.

What we interpret as such is disturbance in the manifestation and not in the power itself.

Thought currents passing from God to man and from Mind to mind are charged with power in the Silence. When we learn to make connection with our source, we shall learn that Ask and ye shall receive is not only a Scriptural quotation but a metaphysical fact.

Say often as you go about your daily task—

GOD KNOWS HIMSELF AND KNOWS ME AS HIMSELF. I TOO KNOW MYSELF AS GOD TROUGH THIS MUTUAL KNOWING. I HAVE SPIRITUAL POWER. I AM FULLY CONSCIOUS OF THIS POWER. I ACCEPT MY AWARENESS OF IT GRATEFULLY. I AM ACTING IN THIS CONSCIOUSNESS AND AWARENESS NOW.

Emerson says, "As soon as the man is one with God, he will not beg. He will then see prayer in all action. The prayer of the farmer kneeling in his field to weed it, the prayer of the rower kneeling with the stroke of his oar, are true prayer heard throughout nature, though for cheap ends." Wherever there is a need, there is a prayer. It is a conscious or unconscious reaching out to the source for supply. The whole Infinite Universe is sustained by an incessant prayer, by demand and supply. Life cannot live apart from its Source. Even the primrose by the dusty road prays to the earth, the sun and the air. It demands the elements which are necessary for its unfoldment, and the prayer is fulfilled.

When the man outside merges with the Man Inside, he knows himself to be not only the prayer but the answer also. As man feels this Divinity stirring and as It reaches forth to control his subjective life, Silence will become a part of his everyday living. But it must not become merely a means of receiving loaves and fishes. The I AM is indifferent to things because it recognizes nothing apart from Itself. It desires only man's unity with Itself. In this unity man embodies his Good. In the intangible world of Spirit, all things needful to man are classified under the heading of Good. If we seek the supremacy of Good (God), we shall never lack. Not until we withdraw our thought from the relative plane are we able to cultivate our inner resources.

As we center in the formless presence of God and become responsive only to that which is Good, two things will happen. We shall know sensations never before experienced and shall emerge with definite guidance or leading. In praying, we talk to God and his answer comes in the form of inspiration. The voice of Intuition that speaks in the Silence is the infallible Word of God.

The intuitive faculty is by far the most valuable and yet the most delicate instrument of Mind. It is the guiding force of the Soul. But unless we search for it with great patience and are obedient to its slightest prompting, we shall miss it. It is the still small voice of the I AM.

Robert A. Russell

Chapter 3
Principles of The Silence

We are living in an era of research, an era of applied science. Man today has developed to the point at which he can make use of forces that have existed since time began. It is a period marked by a revival of interest in religion, and particularly in the power of faith to heal.

Much of our religion has been cold, dull, stodgy, vague and idealistic. It has not only diverted the teachings of Jesus from their practical application to a superstition and miraculous belief, but it has shut out their true import. Without enthusiasm, without inspiration, without the glad assurance of a living faith, it has been of little value in equipping men to meet the ills, problems and vicissitudes of human life.

In the Silence a vast, unexplored field of spiritual research is waiting for those who seek a larger experience of God. Man's relationship to the Universe is still imperfectly and incompletely understood.

Jesus said, Seek and ye shall find; knock and it shall be opened unto you; ask and ye shall receive. Have you not often wondered what is implied in these commands? What is it that we shall find if we seek? What is it that shall open to us if we knock? What is it we shall receive if we ask? There are perfectly natural questions which can be answered only by those who have sought, knocked and received.

All through the age there have been those who have found God, who have entered the door of Reality, who have received their Good. This experience is possible of attainment to every living soul.

We long for permanency, for conscious unity with God. We long for freedom from the disasters, perplexities, illnesses and disappointments of a changing world. To secure these blessings, we must have contact with the Higher Life that seeks avenues of expression through us. We must develop receptivity to the spiritual impulses which make us free.

The way to immunize ourselves from the lesser things of life and to open ourselves to the greater ones is the way of Silence. Silence encompasses the Infinities of God, and opens the door to our conscious realization that God is One, God is All, and God is Good; that everything is under the dominion of His Mind; that the Soul is one with and inseparable from the Universal Soul; that God's Mind and our Consciousness are one, that the Principle of Life is harmonious in its expression to the extent that the individual Mind is controlled and guided by the Universal Mind.

The first Principle announced by those who have had the larger experience of God in the Silence is that we are surrounded by an Infinite Intelligence, or Mind, which meets us at the level of our own comprehension of ourselves; that it responds to us by corresponding with our state of thought.

When we have entered the Inner Chamber and are no longer conscious of the body or of limitation of any sort but are conscious only of being conscious, Divine Mind responds to us to the degree that we accept it as one with our own Mind. We enter into the Consciousness of God in such degree as we comprehend that the Universal Mind and our consciousness are One. Only as we shut off the flow of our personal thought do we enter the Divine Presence and identify ourselves with the Universal Mind. The purpose of the Silence is to unify the individual Mind and the Universal Mind. The more complete our comprehension that all Good is under the dominion of our own Mind, the greater will be its expression in our lives.

When we have elevated the individual Mind to the Universal Mind, we shall discover for the first time the full meaning of Omnipresence, Omnipotence and Omniscience; we shall discover that we are self-sustained, self-maintained, self-governed, and that we do not have to struggle to become that which we already are.

To the degree that we realize this, there is response from the Universal Mind. Spirit embodies Itself in our thought and moves from this center to the circumference of our physical activities. Our intelligence is of the same nature as that of Universal Intelligence. It contains everything within Itself. When we have arrived at a state of spiritual realization through which we can consciously approach It, believe in It, and receive It, we automatically control the circumstances of our lives.

As the Spiritual Will or Intent is awakened, the Will that is in accord with Divine Mind, the Law of Spirit serves us. This Law knows only one method, but it is so perfect that It never contradicts Itself or makes a mistake.

Not my will, but thine, be done. With the Spiritual Will in conscious control directing all the faculties of the mind, the individual will accomplish everything he undertakes. The promise of every demonstration already exists within the mind that is completely identified with God. Uncertainty gives way to certainty, complexity become simplicity, and problems are unerringly solved. Therefore take unto you the whole armour of God, that ye may be able to withstand in the evil day, and having done all to stand. The whole armour is symbolical of the awakened Consciousness, which knows One God and only one; One Cause, and only one. To this God every consciousness has access, for It is in every mind.

The final and complete emancipation from human limitation and false beliefs is to lose all sense of two powers, to see only Good. Ye shall know the truth, and the truth shall make you free. Knowledge is the natural precedent to freedom. Man's only responsibility is to know; Truth's only responsibility is to free him. When we perceive the true idea of God, Truth will set the law in motion. The Universal Mind responds to the individual idea, and the Law creates by correspondence with the idea.

I am come that ye might have life and have it more abundantly. The abundance that we express is always commensurate with our recognition of the Law (God). The greatest good that can come to man is the realization of the full and complete Spirit of Good within himself.

All seeking must be based on the fundamental principle that God is Wholeness and Completion; that He is Mind, Intelligence and Life ; that as a man thinketh in his heart (Soul, Mind), so is he. The creative medium of God is His thought. The creative medium of man is his thought. Freedom and bondage are both in the Law of Mind. Negative thinking produces bondage. Positive thinking produces freedom. Negative thinking is thought not consistent with the essential goodness and wholeness of God.

The Law of Mind fulfills the idea but does not know the difference between health and sickness, harmony and inharmony, prosperity and poverty. It does not even know one mind from another. It does not know what to do but only how to do. Its purpose is to establish the word, and to execute the idea which is contained in the word. All freedom and all bondage are in the Law. It brings into our experience that which we impress upon our subconscious mind.

If our thinking is consistent with what we really desire, we are using the Law constructively. If, on the other hand our thinking is inconsistent, we are using it destructively; in either case, the unknowing and impersonal Law establishes the word that we have sent forth.

Seek the Truth, and you shall find It. Command the Truth, and It will respond to you. The Truth is real; what is not Truth is not real. The Truth about man is that he is a living Soul expressing God. He is Perfect Man, made in the mental or spiritual image and likeness of God. The Spirit itself beareth witness with our spirit, that we are the children of God. Truth forever declares the perfection of God in man. God is Intelligence, and man-made in the image and likeness of God shares the same Intelligence. When man awakens to the fact that his intelligence is God-Intelligence and that his consciousness is God-Consciousness, there is no problem he cannot solve, no obstacle he cannot overcome, and no goal which he cannot reach. The challenge to man is to discover and express that which is inherently within himself.

When the Truth is known, it is instantly demonstrated; the only Truth we can ever know is that which may be known right now. Beloved, now are we the sons of God. Perfection in all things exists now; as It is revealed to us in the Silence, It is brought into manifestation. In this realization, we discover that there is nothing to heal, for nothing ever gets sick but man's thought of himself. The Principle of Perfection cannot create that which is imperfect. If God is perfect, His idea and manifestation must be perfect.

The Silence is the Kingdom of God. It is the realm above and beyond all friction which the Psalmist called a large place; It is a place of life, spontaneity and mighty realization. The Lord is in his holy temple; let all the earth keep silence before him. This temple is in the vast reaches of mind, and our worship is communion, a conscious identity with God, a union conferring peace, poise, joy, freedom, and inward quickening. Those who find and dwell in this place are sheltered and protected by the eternal shadow of the Almighty.

Peter speaks of the hidden man of the heart. There are many references to the place of Silence in the Christian as well as other Scriptures, the common term for it being the heart, which is the soul or subjective mind. We are to serve God with the wholeheart, we are to love Him with the whole heart. Our concept is enlarged as we meditate upon the word as we find it in such combinations as these: God is the strength of my heart... Let not your heart be troubled... Thy wordhave I hid in my heart... A man's heart deviseth his way... the treasure of the heart... the pure in heart. We possess God in the heart or soul, and we realize Him in the Silence. This is the meaning of Pascal's statement, "Thou coulds't not seek me hadst thou not already found me," Because God is, man may experience the grandeur and dignity of His Being in his own mind. Lifting our vision from the form to the Formless, we can find and experience the eternal values of the Soul.

God Works Through Silence

We should always enter the Silence in faith. We must emerge in the conscious knowledge that whatever claims we make there have been met. Whoever enters the Silence with an open and receptive mind receives. But we must be emptied before we can be filled. We must relinquish all specific thoughts or emotional responses to the external world. We must be open to Spiritual impulses. The mind that receives must be en rapport with the Mind that gives.

We should always leave the Silence with praise and thanksgiving. I thank thee, Father, that thou hast heard me is a triumphant recognition of the law of cause and effect. I know that thou hearest me always. We do not beg, beseech nor implore. We know. If the faith we took into the Silence remains unimpaired, we can demand the utmost that God can give.

Now are we the sons of God—not next week or next month, but NOW! NOW is the only moment that is eternal. It is the only one in which we can actually live and function. Since all activity is in the present moment, everything that God is must be translated into the present moment. The present moment never ends; what is not already present can never be demonstrated. God's work is finished.

Whether our response from the Silence is in language readily understood, in symbols that must be interpreted, or in terms of some prompting through the senses, it must be appropriated in the present moment.

Judge Troward says, "The conception of spirit as pure thought, and not as concrete form, is the conception of it as subsisting perfectly independently of the elements of time and space.... When the elements of time and space are eliminated all our ideas of things must necessarily be as subsisting in a universal here and an everlasting now."

Chapter 4
The Principle of Universal Mind

In the great Silence of the Soul, there is power; power to achieve; power to visualize; power to pray; power to realize; the power to know. The Spirit of man lives and moves in the Cosmic Silence; it is there that the creative mind grasps the power to materialize the likeness of that which it can see. "Order is heaven's first law." As the mind looks inwardly into the vastness of God, it will begin to move in orderly and serene fashion. In the Silence, the mind localizes on one idea. This one idea, working through the Law of Attraction and having the power of fulfillment within itself, fashions a form for itself out of the substance of the Silence. Then as the Universal Substance flows into the form, it appears in our objective life as a personal experience.

The Substance of the Silence is the basic element in which all things grow before they appear on the earth. It is that element of the soul in which we plant the seed-ideas that the Creative Power of Mind fashions into forms.

As the mind penetrates more deeply into the realm of the Silence in which God dwells in the fullness of His majesty, all power is given and all things are known, a deep and almost overpowering sense of stillness will pervade the entire field of consciousness.

As consciousness will journey in any direction which the mind gives it, the higher we raise the consciousness, the more invincible our thought and ideas become. God always meets man at the level of his own understanding. As man enters the Consciousness of God, he must eliminate all belief in limitation, separation, time and space. The Universal Mind of God is unlimited, timeless and spaceless. Mind is everywhere present, knows all, sees all, and controls all. In the Silence, consciousness strikes deeper and deeper into that marvelous realm in which all Substance and all Power await.

The power of the word is in the depths of the Soul. It becomes creative only as it is placed with great feeling in the depths of the Universal Mind. The possibilities of any constructive word charged with the enormous power of God is beyond human comprehension. Such a word can perform miracles. The reach of any word spoken in the Consciousness of the One Power is unlimited, and the more positive the word, the greater its power. When the mind is positive, everything works in harmony with the object in view. When the mind is divided, the energy is scattered, and consciousness becomes like a river that sends its water into many small, weak and shallow streams. To be a power, the water (energy) of the river of consciousness must be kept in one course. The negative never attracts the constructive.

There are three levels of consciousness through which the Creative Mind acts.

CONSCIOUS MIND (mental activity)

The conscious mind is the ordinary world consciousness, the working mind by which we cognize and commonly think. It is related to our ordinary states of consciousness and perceives by means of the senses.

SUBCONSCIOUS MIND (subjective activity)

The subconscious, or subjective mind, is the Creative Self-Consciousness of the soul. It is compelled to receive and act upon the thought that reaches it. It obeys the will of the conscious mind. It is a blind force, always obedient to the Spirit.

I AM (Spirit; the Spiritual Self)

I AM is the Super Mind, the sum total of God-Consciousness; the action of this mind is always within and upon Itself. It is the complement of the other two minds and the container of both. The three in reality are one.

There is only one mind, the Universal Mind of God. Mind and Consciousness are interchangeable terms. Conscious and sub-conscious are two names for the One Mind. Subconscious and subjective mean the same thing—the mind and the law of the soul.

Unlimited power is available to man as he consciously uses the creative force. The I AM which we discover in our own consciousness is the Principle we use in our work in the Silence. Both conscious and subjective minds are the instruments of the I AM.

I AM is the perfect and full expression of invisible Spirit. It is the Universal Mind in action. I AM is health. I AM is prosperity. I AM is success. The I AM is the Principle and Power of God and the invisible power of man.

What we call your mind and my mind are two manifestations or expressions of the One Mind. We do not say you have "an air" and I have "an air," or that a fish has "a water." There is one water in which fishes live; one air which we breathe; one Mind of which we are all a part.

I AM is the Omnipresent, Universal Mind of God. It is the Principle of divine Unity underlying all creation; when Self-conscious in man. There is no separation in Spirit; the individual mind can never be separated from the Universal Mind.

I AM is Universal Mind.
I AM is Life.
I AM is Power.
I AM is Health.
I AM is Wealth.
I AM is Success.
I AM is Everything I am or can be, for
I AM the I AM!

To him that hath (the consciousness of I AM) shall be given; to him that hath not shall be taken away even that which he hath. It is one thing to say that we believe in God and quite another to be conscious of God.

When we speak of the Universal Mind, we mean the Omnipresent Consciousness of God, the One Mind which inheres in all things, whose activity is Universal. Omnipresence completely fills the Universe. Everything is filled with the Principle of Life. Since His consciousness is our consciousness, we lack nothing. Mind is everywhere; there is no place where God is not.

Man is a conscious, willing, thinking, knowing center of the Universal Mind of God. The I AM reacts to him according to the sum total of his beliefs. Man is Universal on the subjective side of life, and individual at the point of conscious perception. The individual uses the creative power of the Universal Mind every time he uses his own mind.

Mind is everywhere, in everything and through everything: everything can respond to our thought. Jesus revealed this Truth when He spoke to the fig tree, saying, Bear no more fruit, henceforth; when He spoke to the winds and commanded them to be peaceful. When a unity has been established between the individual and the Universal I AM, Mind Substance can be directed into any channel.

The Universal Mind is always impersonal. It never decides who shall use it. It becomes personal only as It expresses through us. It doesn't matter who we are, or what we are. The sun shines on the good and the evil, and the rain falls on the just and the unjust. God is accessible and responsive to all.

Cast thy bread upon the waters, for thou shalt find it after many days. The Law is exact. Thoughts are things, and things are thoughts. Cast your thought into the Universal Mind, and in due time it will return as form.

"Which of you, when asked by his son for a loaf, will hand him a stone? Or, if he asks for fish, will you hand him a serpent? Well, if for all your evil you know to give your children what is good, how much more will your Father in heaven give good to those who ask him?"

The Perfect Mind honors our faith in it. It is always orderly and exact. The thought of bread produces bread. The thought of fish produces fish. But if we expect a stone, we shall get that too. If our thoughts are sick, we get sickness. There are many ways of using the power, but only one Law. By thy words thou shalt be justified, and by thy words thou shalt be condemned.

There is no limitation nor competition in Universal Creative Mind. In the Silence, we identify ourselves with It, recognize in It the good we desire, and let It work for us. Mind penetrates everything; It does not know the barriers of space and time. We do not send out thoughts, for there is nowhere to send them. There is only One Mind to send them. There is only One Mind to think about us, only One Mind by which we think. To be conscious of Universal Mind is to be conscious of Reality.

The Universal Mind is the Self-Conscious, Self-Knowing, purposeful activity of Spirit. It is at work everywhere and in everything. Even the lowest forms of life reveal the Omnipresent Mind at work. The moneron, the lowest form of independent life, is a perfect model in miniature of our modern submarine. As it inflates and deflates its body in order to rise and sink in the water, it betrays a wonderful intelligence. The spider and the bee show engineering skill that is amazing. The dahlia knows that it must store up starch for the winter while it is growing in the summer. Mind is at work everywhere. It becomes the Consciousness of whatever it contacts. The tree, flower and blade of grass are alive with the Consciousness and Substance of the Universal Mind of God. It is the color, perfume, life and beauty of everything that is. It is the medium through which man comes ultimately to know the truth.

Spiritual energy comes from within. The I AM is the source of Divine Energy. It flows through the consciousness of man as an impersonal, silent and Omnipresent Power. Through his soul (subjective mind), man makes his conscious approach to the Universal Mind. To be conscious of It is to be in vital touch with It, to give It conscious direction in body and affairs.

Mind meets us at the level of our own understanding and manifests according to our consciousness. Since It cannot give us more than we can receive, we must be consciously receptive to It. Our work in the Silence is dynamic, the results differing according to our various states of consciousness.

The I AM in us is the only God we shall ever know. If we recognize It and accept It as health, It will manifest as an abundant health. If we recognize It and accept It as happiness, It will manifest as abundant happiness. If we recognize It and accept It as opulence, It will manifest as abundant prosperity. As we release this Divine Energy, It will become to us anything we believe It to be. Since we actually live and move in this Energy, there can be no thought of bringing God down to us from some high place in the sky, but rather of lifting our thought to the heavenly place in our own minds in which we may more fully comprehend Him.

In the Silence, we cultivate a deep consciousness of unity with the Universal Creative Mind. We merge with It until It becomes our own Consciousness. We take from It as much as we are prepared to receive.

FRIEND, GO UP HIGHER!

Robert A. Russell

Chapter 5
The One Mind Active Through Man

We have learned that the discovery of God has to be linked up inevitably with Self-discovery, that the Universe in which we live is spiritual and not material, that there is only One Mind, to which time and space are nothing, and that this Mind of God is really our Mind. We learned, too, that there is one Substance—the Substance of our own mind—which is always active in the soul and ready to take form on the surface. Since the whole process through which the I AM works is one of consciousness, one must look to consciousness for everything needful in his life. Man is solely dependent upon himself— upon his own consciousness and the power of his own Mind. He becomes masterful to the degree that he is able to harmonize his consciousness with his own divine Mind and to recognize that Mind is the Substance of all things. Mind does not become things; It is things.

The thought which we must keep in mind is that God Consciousness does not change or add anything to us. Our only purpose is to reveal the Life Principle and Power of the Universal Mind, God. When we treat, or attempt to move negative conditions such as disease and poverty, we are recognizing two powers and binding the negative conditions to us. We are unconsciously admitting that the good we seek does not exist. Jesus said, I am come not to destroy, but to fulfill. Even a thought about lack, or a desire to add substance to ourselves, is to discredit the Mind which is the Substance of all things. The positive qualities of the I AM will always become visible when we drop from our consciousness the belief in the negative qualities.

Creation is finished and perfect. There is actually nothing to heal or be added from the outside. God is that which I AM; my purpose is not to demonstrate things, but to reveal, or to give out from my Center, what that Center is. I can do that only by keeping myself in absolute harmony with that which I AM. Acknowledge him in all the ways. I am saved from all untoward circumstances only by virtue of what I AM, by the Life Principle of the Universal Mind. I AM the way, the truth and the life. My mission is to cooperate with the Universal Consciousness in my own mind. The circumstances of my life will automatically express the harmonious action of my thought.

Any attempt to move anything out of the body or the circumstances, anything which does not have a cause in Divine Mind, will nullify the demonstration. Disagreeable conditions have no existence whatever outside of consciousness; therefore we must look to our own thoughts for a solution of our problems. The human body and the body of one's affairs will automatically express the prevailing state of thought in the mind.

When we discover that our Mind is the Mind of God, that His Power is our Power, we shall be so close to Him that He will be in everything we do. When the I AM is given dominion over our consciousness, it works perfectly. Realizing this, we can walk perfectly, hear perfectly and see perfectly. Let this mind be in you.

Freedom is assured when we let go of the personal sense, the consciousness of the body which we have so long separated from the Universal Mind of God. To tell a blind man that he can see, or a lame man that he can walk, is the truth of the Omnipresent Self. He may desire to know this, try to imagine or pray that it is so, but until he is conscious only of the I AM within him as the center of his sight or his walking, nothing will happen.

When one is absolutely relaxed, conscious only of being conscious, when he has taken his attention away from himself and from his world and fixed his attention only upon the I AM within him, he will be in tune with everything in the Universe and have dominion over it.

Behold, I am He that should come... And the government shall be upon his shoulders. The Presence that will finally rule our lives is now offering a full salvation through our consciousness; but flesh and blood cannot inherit the kingdom. Whilst we are at home in the body (material thought), we are absent from the Lord. All flesh must be spiritualized. We must surrender all ideas of bondage.

Our senses are really God's senses; when we realize this, we cannot have poor eyesight, poor hearing, poor health or poor anything. I AM sees through our eyes, hears through our ears, thinks through our minds, works through our bodies. He is All-in-All. I AM declares health and power in every corpuscle, every vein, every cell, every nerve and every atom of the body saying unto them, Be ye therefore perfect even as your Father in heaven is perfect. I AM will fill the body to overflowing with Divine power and Health, for I AM is within every cell, and every cell is alive with the Universal Substance of I AM.

When he, the Spirit of truth, has come, he will guide you into all truth. The Spirit of Truth is the I AM of the Universal Mind. When man recognizes that his consciousness is One with the I AM Consciousness, the recognition will guide him into all Truth. We cannot change the truth, but we can change the manifestation of the Law.

There is no lack of substance in the great Universal Mind of God, but it is impersonal. Man can always enter the stream of this Universal Substance through the Intelligence and Power of his own I AM, but he can never approach it through the personality or human intellect. Only by surrendering the finite belief in a personal mind and personal self and personal desire that continually tries to demonstrate substance, is it possible to enter the very Substance Itself.

He that losses his life shall find it in the Universal Source. The only thing that can be lost (set aside) are the false belief of the limited personal self. Divine Substance and Power cannot function in a divided or personal consciousness. The mind must be One and the attitude impersonal before we can experience the Power. Greater is he that is in you than he that is in the world. The Impersonal Life is the I AM or spiritual consciousness, which says, If any man will come after me, let him deny himself and take up his cross daily. The cross represents the Universal Mind of God through which the false beliefs of personal consciousness are denied or set aside by the God Consciousness. By lifting one's thought to the Universal Mind, one crosses out all that is opposed to or at variance with God.

Be ye transformed by the renewing of your mind. The Truth can only be known as the entire consciousness is surrendered to the Universal Mind which is Oneness, Wholeness and Completeness. The Law must be fulfilled in our consciousness by the clear perception that God is all. Merely thinking the Truth never changes anyone. It is the conscious knowing of the Truth that changes man from a material to a spiritual basis. Knowing the Truth means to have the true idea of Principle or God and the true idea of man.

The word Principle used so frequently in our lessons means the Law of God — the I AM, Universal Mind, Spiritual Substance, the Omnipresent, Omnipotence and Omniscience of our own Minds. One cannot think of the word Principle without losing the thought of the personal. Since the true nature of God is impersonal, the word will gradually clear the concept of a personal God subject to all the limitations which personality connotes.

As we vibrate (think) in the Universal Mind, we have the consciousness of unity. The stronger our consciousness the more we are able to receive. A simple illustration will make this point clear. A piece of ice is placed in a glass of water. The atoms of ice, as we know, are vibrating at a low rate; the atoms of water are vibrating at a higher rate. If the ice is allowed to remain in the water long enough it will melt, and after a time it will be water. The ice disappears (as ice) and is changed back to water because the rate of its vibration is increased. All the atoms in the glass then vibrate at the same rate.

Vibration is at the base of all form; it is independent of physical force. When we learn how to vibrate consciously in the Universal Mind, we shall know that we are one with the substance of I AM. The highest vibrations and the greatest power are silent. When we enter the Silence, we change our rate of vibration from the slow and negative to the fast and positive. We lose our sense of the personal as we merge with the impersonal I AM.

Ye shall receive power when the Holy Spirit is come upon you. When we become one with Spirit, Spirit enters into us and we enter into it. It manifests through us as perfect being.

Let there be Light. God thought and wrought. Then Word was spoken, that which was authoritatively affirmed was done, and there was Light.

It makes little difference whether we review this record of Creation as allegory or actuality, as spiritual or material, as fable or fact. Something within us responds, and we are led to rational and helpful deductions. Consciousness becomes clear, and through this crystal we see the spectrum of that Light which needs no record to prove that it is a manifestation of God. It is the Light in which we see Light. We see friendliness, compassion, helpfulness, love, service, truth, faith, harmony, peace, hope, wisdom, plenty, and these attributes reveal the Life more abundant. They reveal God! Creation!

Instead of dismissing the formless void from thought, the Creator projected into it the illumination of the Light of His Mind, and behold! there was the somethingness called Earth with its color, wealth, beauty, grandeur, its utility and possibilities for the habitation of mankind, and the vastness of the starry depths of Space.

Is it not significant that all the days of God's creating are, according to the record, made of first an evening and then a morning? From the twilight, to the mists, and the seeming absence of Light to the awakening dawn and the beauty and glory of noon's effulgence? The day is commenced and done in the glorious illumination of Infinite Mind.

Subsequently came One whose teachings bear witness to the light. The Light which was discerned, even in degree, could never be completely extinguished. Mankind might, and from its limited viewpoint would, seek more Light, but never again would it be lost to man in an unutterable darkness of the formless void. When the Great Light shone, the darkness disappeared forever; and the Light of the World is seen to be the Light of our Life.

Everything was created by the illumined Word and everything thus created was Good. The Word defined cannot be disassociated from Right Ideas; and the Word realized in Right Action gives man dominion.

In the main, unexpressed ideas are of as little value to mankind as is their expression without realization. Expression is a necessary preliminary to that realization which is the dominion of Right Ideas. Your expression, whether in character or in performance, is the responsibility that you owe to the rest of your world for your awareness of the power, ability and strength that the radiant energy of the Light bestows upon you.

You receive Light that you, too, may bear witness to the Light; and this is a duty you owe to God and to man made in his image. You are unfaithful steward if you leave right ideas in the Silence, if you do not act upon them and bring them into useful service.

The Way is revealed to us through the Right Ideas which come in the Silence. Such ideas are mental representations of possible realities; they are mental pictures of circumstances and conditions, or projects of things we desire, purpose of plan which are capable of being realized.

You will find that the Infinite Light, which is the reflection of God, still illumines the dark places of the earth, and that it is the True Light that lights every willing man in the way wherein he should go.

But there is a Spirit in man; and the inspiration of the Almighty giveth them understanding."Speak to Him thou for He hears, and Spirit with Spirit can meet—Closer is He than breathing, and nearer than hands and feet.

Part Two
God's Workshop
The Mechanics of Silence

Chapter 1
Relaxation

Enter into thy closet, and when thou hast shut the door, pray to thy Father, which is in secret, and thy Father who seeth in secret shall reward thee openly.

When Jesus gave these directions for prayer, He said all that could be said about the right method of prayer. Only as the personal mind is stilled and thought and attention are withdrawn from the outer world can the consciousness enter the deep rhythm and harmony of the Eternal Soul.

The word closet implies seclusion and exclusion. We think of it as a room by itself, a closed room without window, and with only one door for the entrance. The closet here referred to is Within, the innermost chamber of the Universal Mind.

But around this door are assembled multitudes of disturbing thoughts and negative distractions pressing their claims for admittance. Jesus said, shut the door. We enter the Silence through silence; it can never be entered through discord, division or confusion. In quietness and confidence shall be thy strength. Be still and know that I AM God.

In the Silence, we must be insensitive to everything but the Voice Within; the senses must be unresponsive to the voices of the material world. Until the physical and intellectual machinery is stopped, the Inner Voice will not speak. The Lord is in his holy temple; let all the earth keep silence before him. Silence begins where stillness leaves off. They are not the same thing; one may be absolutely still in body and mind, and not be in Silence. Stillness is only a preparation for the Silence.

The purpose in the Silence is to quiet the intellectual voices from the outer world, and to gather all one's faculties and powers into one focal point in the soul.

We must empty ourselves before we can be filled. We must relinquish all intruding thoughts from the outer world by withdrawing our thought and attention from them. If one give attention to his thoughts and tries to eliminate them by force of will, he sets up a resistance and turns his thoughts outwardly instead of inwardly. He fixes his attention upon the without instead of the Within, and he still functions on the surface. To shut the door, the consciousness must be directed to the Within.

There is never any effort in the Silence. Effort is always denial of the God who is still. When the whole attention is concentrated upon the peaceful Within, all the action of the mind becomes serene. This one thing I do.

It is impossible to make the mind a blank and go on living at the same time. To stop thinking is to stop living, and we cannot suspend consciousness as long as we are conscious of being conscious. Neither can we think of nothing, for to think of nothing is to think of something. In the Silence we are working with Intelligence, and we must meet it intelligently; we must be definite and positive to one idea at a time. Our thought should center upon the Absolute without the anxiety, fear, or any sense of pressure or force. If thine eye be single, thy whole body shall be full of light.

There are and always have been persons in whom the sense of Oneness with God is uninterrupted. They intuitively communicate with Him without formality of any kind. They were so aware that they live and move and have their being in Him that they are sensitized only to the world of the Spirit, to Reality. They have no need of the discipline that most of us must undergo before we are fully aware of His nearness.

Relaxation is a discipline which one must impose upon the mind and body in order to reach the Silence. The body is a complex and wonderful machine which needs decarbonizing just as a mechanical engine does. There is a vital force in every breath we take which can clean and purify the physical man. The mind affects the breathing, and the breathing in turn affects the body. We know that if our thinking is deep and calm, the breathing is slow and regular, and if we are nervous and agitated, the breathing is jerky and irregular. Right breathing stimulates perception, peace of mind, intuition and awareness.

We are living in an age of speed and there are really few people in this hectic civilization who take time to live. They hurry from morning until night; they bolt their food and live in a veritable whirlwind. When the body rises up to condemn them, they wonder why.

In an old bicycle era, there was a familiar phrase, "riding on the rims." The wise man does not ride on flat tires, not only because of the great discomfort but because it is bad for the tires and expensive. Those who live on their nerves find the road of life ragged and rough. They are like yesterday's lettuce, but lettuce can be revitalized and made alive by plunging it into water. If it is allowed to remain there for a long enough period of time, it becomes firm and fresh. So it is with an over strong and frayed body. By plunging it into the crystal water of Life, one can draw from the Universe a new resiliency and freshness. Through relaxation, one can become receptive to the all-pervading and renewing power of God.

The body can be trained to obey the command of the mind and by practice, you will find that the muscles will let go as you speak directly to them and give the order, "Relax!" Assume a comfortable position. Free yourself of anything that binds or restricts your body in any way. Breathe deeply and regularly. Direct your thought to any specific part of the body that has not responded. Tense muscles inhibit free action of Mind through you. Use the word Peace to further the letting go of the human mind as well as of the body. Routine is more readily established if the time and place of your practice are kept the same.

Chapter 2
Concentration

When you have completely given the body over to God and it is free, easy and silent, you are ready to step into that new dimension of mind—the Silence. You are entering the divine Presence of the I AM. You are approaching the state of consciousness that unifies with Intelligence, Power, Substance, Wisdom, Life and Love. Your vision and thought must be single to the I AM in the realization that there is nothing but God.

By staying the mind upon your own I AM, you absorb something of the spiritual environment which you have entered. Your nature takes on the Divine Nature. The beginner in this work will find that the door to the closet will fly open many times during this period and that many unwelcome thoughts will knock. Do not arouse yourself to resist them. Dismiss them by saying something like this, "Go away now. This is not your time or place. If you are important, I'll think about you later."

It is a good practice to begin the Silence with the Lord's Prayer, concentrating upon the meaning of each phrase.

Our Father which art in heaven, Hallowed be thy name.
Thy kingdom come,

Thy will be done in earth as it is in heaven. Give us this day our daily bread,

And forgive us our debts, as we forgive our debtors.

And lead us not into temptation, but deliver us from evil. Amen.

OUR FATHER WHICH ART IN HEAVEN

The first word of the Lord's prayer is inclusive of everything that is contained in the Universe. Our Father is a declaration of our sonship; in these words you are claiming for everyone the blessings which you are seeking for yourself. That "a prayer for less than the all-good is vicious" is a recognized metaphysical truth. Where the Divine Presence is, there is Heaven. The Kingdom of Heaven is within you. Everything comes to you in a Silence through your recognition of the Father's Presence within yourself.

Our Father who art in Heaven literally means, "My God, within my own mind."

HALLOWED BE THY NAME

The word hallow means to consecrate, to devote to sacred purposes, to revere. Name is an appellation or designation. In His name or nature, you enter the Consciousness of God. Hallowed be thy name is an absolute recognition of the Divine Mind—which is your Mind. In these words, you accept your divine heritage as a child of God.

THY KINGDOM COME

The Kingdom is come; it is established here and now. The good which you seek is already here. Be conscious of it. Recognize it. Unify yourself with it. Know that you are established in the Consciousness of Perfection and Harmony.

THY WILL BE DONE IN EARTH AS IT IS IN HEAVEN

Surrender your human will to the Divine Will that you may think and receive only that which is good. Know that the Law of the Universal Mind is the Law of your personal mind, that your subjective mind is one with the heavenly Mind.

GIVE US THIS DAY OUR DAILY BREAD

The bread spoken of here refers not alone to food, clothing and money, but to the Bread of Life. Man shall not live by bread alone, but by every word that proceedeth out of the mouth of God. The law of increased is in the word. I AM is the active agent of creation. It externalizes itself in the substance that co-exists with it. I am the bread of life.

Give us this day our daily bread. These words literally mean to you, "I am positive to the Substance of the I AM here and now. I am receptive to It. My needs are met." The word give is a command to Substance. You are not begging, pleading or beseeching. You are affirming the Truth, identifying yourself with It and accepting It.

FORGIVE US OUR DEBTS AS WE FORGIVE OUR DEBTORS

One of the tests of sonship is the ability to forgive not only others but one's self as well. Blessed are the pure in heart. Any bitterness, condemnation, vengeance, criticism or malice in the consciousness nullifies the harmony you are trying to achieve. The Law will not work until you have forgiven everybody for everything. There is no forgiveness without forgetfulness. Until you let go of that which is undesirable, you cannot receive that which is desirable.

When you forgive yourself and others, you open the door of your consciousness so that good may enter.

LEAD US NOT INTO TEMPTATION, BUT DELIVER US FROM EVIL

Evil is only a false belief about God. These words actually mean, "Lead us safely through all temptation to recognize two powers, and deliver us from all false beliefs." Be positive to the Law of Good and negative to all limited conditions and appearances. Recognize the Presence as the only Reality.

AMEN

Jesus concluded the prayer with the oldest word in our possession. Amen. The word is actually the sacred name for the Power back of all creation and means literally, The Hidden One. Amen is really the cohesive force of any prayer. It is a word that precipitates immediate expression. It clinches and vitalizes all other affirmations. It sets the Universal Forces into activity. Amen should be used after every affirmation and prayer, and be thought of as the Power of the I AM (Spirit) to impregnate substance. Amen is the mighty pronouncement that It is done.

By concentration, you bring your forces to a focus. Wherever there is a great manifestation of power, mechanical, physical or spiritual, there is concentration. Only concentrated power can be directed and controlled. As you work in the Silence, you concentrate on the knowledge that one Substance fills the Universe. God's Life is your Life; God's Mind is your Mind; God's Thought is your Thought; God's Strength is your Strength; God's Substance is your Substance; God's Action is your Action. Concentrate upon this concept of unity you can think from the standpoint of the Whole, until you can think of yourself as One with All. You must accept your function as an inlet and an outlet for Substance and Life.

If thine eye be single, the Scriptures say, "thy whole body shall be full of light." Concentration is singleness of vision and invincibility of purpose. Through concentration, the mind expands and develops, and the scope of consciousness increases.

The thing which you concentrate upon is the thing which draws to yourself.

Your prayers will be answered to the extent that you can hold one thought in Silence to the exclusion of all others. This ability takes time to develop. Do not become discouraged if at first you do not succeed. Give yourself absolutely to the idea in mind. Win it with love. Do not try to force it, do not resent anything unlike it, and do not resist any strangers at the door. Know that this One Idea is your only concern at the present moment. If you feel any tenseness, consciously relax. Treat every encroachment with the word Peace. Your idea will touch the soul and impregnate the Universal Substance only as you give it its freedom. An idea is a living, vibrant thing, and it loves freedom just as much as you do. Loose it and let it go.

With the body at rest and the mind stilled, and both enveloped in the consciousness of peace, choose the word or idea that minister to your particular need. Is it joy, peace, health, power, love, strength? Concentrate your whole thought upon that word. Be steadfast, one-pointed. Allow the word to take full possession of you. Claim it as yours and enter into the nature of it until you feel the pulse and vitality of it. God, the Spiritual Substance of the Universe, will fill every part of your being that is not isolated from the idea. Enlarge your concept of the word. See it in its relationship to everything in your life. Identify yourself with it. Involuntarily you will have entered upon the steps of meditation and visualization. No step is a formality in itself. Each overlaps the other.

Chapter 3
Meditation

Concentration develops clear vision, meditation extends that vision until consciousness becomes sufficiently lucid and vivid to encompass the Spirit within you fully. Meditation is always creative. It is that state of mind in which the universe becomes plastic to your thought. Look at your idea as you would look at a beautiful scene, a mountain, or a ship at sea. Let your attitude be calm and natural—no staring, no frowning, no peering, and no tension. To try to hold an idea in the mind by effort is as absurd as to try to hold a pint of water in your hand. The tighter you grasp it the more you lose. The idea has come to you; it is your property. It has no desire to get away from you, but it does want your attention without tension.

The whole responsibility for the consummation of any idea is in the idea. You are simply the channel through which the idea accomplishes its purpose. The mere repetition of words, affirmations, or statements of Truth will never bring anything into manifestation. It is only as we become the word, idea or thought that our good comes to us. When we become the word that we speak and send it forth under the guidance of the Law, we can have absolute confidence that it will accomplish that whereunto it is sent.

The dictionary tells us that meditation means "to keep the mind in a state of contemplation." In concentration, we rivet our thought upon a word or idea. In meditation, we associate ourselves with the word and speculate as to its nature. We extract the inmost substance of the idea and appropriate it to ourselves. The mind searches out every phase of the idea until its entire nature is encompassed. In this process, we know that Divine Mind is revealing the full meaning and purpose of every word, and that the inmost Substance of the word is entering into our waiting consciousness. Much as the scientist blasts the atom, we blast the shell of every word until we are able to get everything that it holds. As the mind blasts a word, it expands and encompasses more and more of its Truth which is the real essence or Spirit of a word or object. Through meditation, we discover the divinity of everything and realize our Oneness with It.

In the innermost depths of every word, there is a Principle of Power which we call Spirit; this is the real Substance and Presence that we must contact in meditation. We must bring the Substance to the surface of our objective life. Meditation is the attitude of listening to the Spirit of the Word—the Principle of Creation.

If ye abide in me (Principle), and my words abide in you, ye shall ask what ye will and it shall be done unto you... Keep thy heart with all diligence; for out of it are the issues of life. Out of the Principle in any word comes the Substance in material form. For as a man thinketh in his heart, so is he. What you dwell upon in the Silence takes possession of you.

The desire which you take with you into the Silence must be spiritually legal, that is, it must harm no one.

As you meditate within yourself, speak only words of Truth— Spirit-filled words which are a law unto themselves. The law of fulfillment is within every word of Truth. Give no thought or attention to appearances, but give your whole thought to realities. Meditation begins and ends in the Secret Chamber of the soul (subjective mind).

Robert A. Russell

Chapter 4
Visualization

What things so ever ye desire, when ye pray, believe that ye receive them, and ye shall have them.

You have already embarked upon this step. You saw your need or were aware of your problem. Now you see your need met, your problem solved, and yourself as a happy, satisfied person moving in a harmonious, peaceful environment. You may have seen how this end can be brought about and you may not. But that phase of the work is not in your department. You have identified yourself with Intelligence, with the All-Knowing, All-Seeing Creator. Who are you to question the manner in which the action will take place?

Through the imagining power of Divine Mind, Spirit propels Itself into creation. Will power is never creative; to suppose that God had to will things into being would be to suppose an opposite or contending force to God.

The Substance that you have extracted from your original and associated ideas must now be reproduced in form. It must be translated from the invisible into the visible. It must be materialized so that you can possess it in a tangible way. Each step brings you nearer to the object of your desire.

The Universal Substance that you are causing to stand around you idea, whose center is I AM, is permeable, impressible, plastic, retentive and sensitive. The I AM, or Spirit, will vitalize any picture that you visualize. It will draw from the Universal Substance whatever is necessary for its material fulfillment.

The speed with which you make any demonstration will depend entirely upon the clarity of your mental picture. You cannot believe you are going to receive anything until you understand definitely what it is that you are going to receive. You must see the picture that you are presenting to Universal Mind very clearly. Not until your picture is clear do you have a good model or mold. The more perfect your picture, the more perfect your manifestation.

The I AM working through the imagination not only can create but can also control. Imagination is the permanizing force that takes an invisible idea and builds it into form. Jesus was able to explore every negative condition and image it into perfection. The Perfect Man is created in the image of the I AM; through Spiritual vision, you can restore your body to its spiritual purity and perfection.

The Universal Mind gives back to you what you deeply impress upon it. In the Silence, you are working in a spiritual foundry in which Universal Substance takes definite shape. If you are careless in your model or pattern, your product will be imperfect.

As the iron worker pours the molten iron into his sand mold, he knows that it will take the shape of the mold. You must be just as meticulous as he in preparing the mold that you wish Creative Principle to fill and just as certain of the result.

The visualizing and imaging faculties are the transcendent powers that cause the living Substance of God to flow freely, but It will fill only those molds prepared for it.

As you mentally hold your picture in the dark room of the Silence, vigilantly guard against the intrusion of any vagrant thoughts that may distort your image. As your picture is impressed upon your consciousness, it becomes the center of attraction, and the I AM fills it with Substance. It becomes the property of the Universal Mind. At this point of development, Spirit specializes and differentiates your desire.

The power which projects the originating Substance out from Itself is your I AM, and this Substance takes the specific shape which you have given it in your mind. The Universal becomes particular as you recognize that your mind is the particular center through which your I AM is seeking expression in a material sense.

The universal Substance with which you are working in the Silence is the most sensitive Substance in the world. In its native state, it is unformed, but It solidifies or assume any form possible to your belief. It distributes Itself through the visual power of your mind. The I AM sends its Substance into the picture that the directive power of yours will give.

You use your will to train the imagination to see only those things which you wish to experience. The quickest way to blot out an adverse or disastrous thought is to ask yourself this question: Is this what I want to happen?

Things to Remember about Visualizing

1. Make your picture clear and definite.

2. Dismiss any inhibiting thought that tries to enter your stream of consciousness.

3. Consecrate your picture to God.

4. Keep your objective or personal mind in a state of harmonious equilibrium with the Soul, or subjective mind.

5. Let your Good come to you; do not force it. Let go and let God.

6. Confidently and expectantly hold the picture, knowing that the Creative Power of the I AM is arranging the specific circumstances and condition for its manifestation.

Suppose that the object of your demonstration is an automobile. If, while you are in the Silence, you just think of an automobile, you may get any kind of a car. You should know definitely what kind of car you want. Then visualize it in every detail. See the body, the color, the wheels, the tires, hubs, caps, the doors, the hood, the trunk, the hardware, the bumpers, the headlights, the horn, and then mentally enter the car. Sit in the driver's seat, see the interior finish, the light overhead, the back seat, the foot rest, the carpet on the floor, ash trays, handles on the doors, the windows, the locks. Now mentally start the engine and take a ride. See yourself on some specific trip. Make the whole thing as real to your mind possible. Now translate the material thing you have visualized into terms of its quality or purpose (the Spiritual equivalent).

You want an efficient means of transportation. You want beauty to be expressed in everything you have and do. You want to be of service to others. You see all the purposes fulfilled by a new car. You know that the storehouse of Creative Energy is full and overflowing. You know that God is able to do exceedingly abundantly above all that we ask or think.

So you bless your old serviceable car (See it in its true light and be grateful for the service it has given to you.) and you thank God that your present need has already been supplied.

You meditate along these lines until you have a feeling of possession and then you make an end of praying. When you have convinced yourself that what you have said with your lips is true in your heart, you know that the thought is yours no longer but God's. It has reached its destination. You have loosed it and let it go. You have accepted what you have asked for and await the gift with confidence.

You do not question the way or the manner in which it will appear. That phase of the work is not yours. You have freed your desire to fulfill itself under the direction of a Power far wiser than yours, of Love that passeth all understanding.

It is impossible to make mental pictures of abstract qualities such as life, power, strength, goodness and understanding. But you can open your mind to the inmost substance of the word and recognize that your need has been met. You can direct the Substance of the word toward yourself, and it will ultimately develop into physical expression. You can repeat the word until it sets up a quality of vibration that will cause the Substance of the word to fill your whole being with the power which it contains. The power within the heart of the word will then be drawn into the mind and demonstrated in experience.

You can mentally visualize yourself as finding a right location, as being consciously receptive to Divine guidance, as being surrounded by goodness, filled with health and power, as confident the answer to the specific problem is known in Principle and is now being revealed to you. Simply present your desire to the Universal Mind. Expect the accomplishment of that desire. Principle is all power, all health, all wisdom, and all knowledge; It will find the answer to any problem and provide the method and means of any manifestation. The fact that you recognize a need or ask a question is proof that the need has already been met, the question already answered.

Chapter 5
Realization

Realization comes to you at the moment you have established the consciousness of your unity with God, the moment in which you can say, I live, yet not I, but Christ liveth in me.

Realization is largely a matter of feeling as a result of knowing. You rest in a new security. You have a feeling of satisfaction in accomplishment, of joy in achievement. You are at peace, for you know your problem is already solved, your need met, your desire granted.

But the dominant feeling is gratitude. Father, I thank thee that thou hast heard me.

Then like Solomon you make an end of praying.

If you do not emerge from the period devoted to the Silence with a feeling of quiet and confidence, you have proof that some barrier of your own making has kept you from crossing the threshold of the door to the closet.

Go back over your steps. Did you try to enter with a divided mind? Was the world too much with you? Was the evidence of the senses too overpowering?

Do not be discouraged but try again. The barrier is man-made. The door to the Secret Place of the Most High is never closed.

You must listen for the Word of God. By entering the Silence, you have said with Samuel, Speak, Lord, for thy servant heareth. Now your part of the work is to hear the answer, to follow the voice of intuition, to accept the means by which your desire is to be accomplished. Change may come wholly within you or it may come in your environment. New opportunities to serve others may appear. Seize them; act upon them.

Jesus' realization enabled Him to see health instead of sickness, to see plenty instead of lack, to see life instead of death.

Your desire rightly placed in Mind has precedence and power over every other thing in your world. The process of realization is four-fold. You must know that the Universal Mind receives your desire, accepts it, acts upon it, and produces it in form. In quietness and confidence shall be thy strength.

Briefly, there are only three steps to any prayer:

1. Recognition of the Spirit, of Omnipresence, of Omniscience, of Omnipotence.

2. Affirmation of man's place in this spiritual creation, of his power to receive untold blessings; of your individual right and privilege; and of your capacity to receive what you have asked for.

3. Gratitude for awareness of your Oneness with God and for your knowledge that the blessing you desire is already yours.

Unbroken consciousness of the Presence of God is the fulfillment of the command to pray without ceasing.

Our need is to be constantly conscious of our unity with God, to be aware of the Presence Within every single moment. When consciousness and awareness become habitual, realization follows automatically. The moment we aspire to know the Truth, we accept the responsibility involved in attaining this state of consciousness. There is no magic formula by which it can be achieved, but the daily practice of setting aside a definite period devoted to the Silence is a means of strengthening our desire and our receptiveness. The more spiritual out development, the more constantly are we aware that we live and move and have our being in Him.

When this contact is broken, it is possible to restore it in the flash of a second. There is no barrier except that our own human thinking, which tends to be concerned with the evidence of the senses. The concepts of time and space are products of our own thought.

No formula is required to make this entry and none is efficacious in itself. The spiritual understanding developed while using any formula is the real instrument of Power.

Those who find it difficult to enter the closet may profit by following a pattern of procedure in their first experiences, which should be recognized for what it is, a temporary step in strengthening the spiritual faculties. Drill in acquiring any skill is forgotten when one becomes proficient in its use. The typist doesn't have to think of the placement of the letters and symbols on the keyboard, or of the position of her hands. The driver of an automobile forgets the steps in the learning-to-drive process but uses the knowledge he acquired automatically. The period in which learning took place has retreated into the background of experience.

You will find specific exercise to help you open the door to the Silence in the Appendix on pages 60 to 66.

You will discover your own key to the door as you continue your practice. For some persons, the door is opened merely by desire or intent. Others have conditioned themselves to a highly individual means. I think of a friend who visualizes a perfect rose and loses herself in its perfection, of another who precipitates the feeling of being immersed in Power as if it were a warm bath. One member of my parish put the experience which she mentally repeats at will into verse. I use it here with her permission but by her request unsigned.

"That Infinity and I related are
Was taught me by the ocean and a star.
I was lost in the booming, the surging, the roar, Detached by the night from the limiting shore, Freed by the motion, so patterned, unending,
Then the Truth spoke to me, my body transcending. The star and I were suspended in space,
And I knew that God was in this place.
Since that rare and precious moment by the sea, I have known my Oneness with Infinity."

When thou prayest, enter into thy closet (Soul), and when thou hast shut the door (detached yourself from the current of human thought and material beliefs), pray to the Father (Universal Mind) which is in secret; and thy Father which seeth in secret shall reward thee openly (shall cause your desire to be objectified).

Chapter 6
How to Give A Treatment in The Silence

The Silence is the world of Light in which there is no darkness at all. The Light heals, and you are that Light. In the Eternal Silence, you are one with Absolute Divine Mind. In the Infinite activity of that Mind, you are active. In the eternal knowing of Divine Health, you are one with all Health.

In the eternal knowing of Divine Supply, you are one with all Supply. You hold within yourself the Infinitude of peace, harmony, life, power, happiness and love. In an indivisible Being, there is no division. In an unlimited Mind, there can be no limitation.

In the Silence, you are present with the Universal Substance of Creation. You are the image, word and idea which will take form. You are in the Spirit which broods over all living forms. You can Speak the word only and thy servant shall be healed

In the case of the centurion's servant, Jesus sent His word and the servant was healed. The word is your Self-Conscious thought. Jesus sent His thought to the centurion's servant, and that is what you do for another in a treatment.

The whole philosophy of giving a treatment is contained in these words of St. John the Divine:

In the beginning was the Word, and the Word was with God, and the Word was God. The same was in the beginning with God. All things were made by Him; and without Him was not anything made that was made. In Him was life; and the life was the light of men.

IN THE BEGINNING WAS THE WORD,
Right Thought is the cause of creation.

AND THE WORD WAS WITH GOD,
Right Thought is in and from Divine Mind.

AND THE WORD WAS GOD.
Right Thought is never separated from Divine Mind.

THE SAME WAS IN THE BEGINNING WITH GOD.
Right Thought and Divine Mind are co-eternal.

ALL THINGS WERE MADE BY HIM;
Reality is objectified by Right Thought and Divine Mind.

AND WITHOUT HIM WAS NOT ANYTHING MADE THAT WAS MADE.
Without Right Thought, Reality cannot be made to stand forth. That which is Real was made and that which is not real has no foundation in Truth.

IN HIM WAS LIFE;
Right Thought is alive. Eternal Life and the Word are the same thing.

AND THE LIFE WAS THE LIGHT OF MEN.
Right Thought and Divine Mind are our own omnipresent consciousness. All Life and Light are consciousness.

The Word comes first; there can be nothing before thought. In the beginning was the Word. The Creative Mind makes things by thinking Right Thought.

The changeless basis from which every treatment must be given is the realization of Perfect Mind—Perfect Consciousness—Perfect God—Perfect Being. Harmony is the principle upon which the whole of creation rests, and since God is the only Reality, anything unlike God (Good) is unreal.

Disease and problems are not realities but effects which of necessity must have a cause. When the cause is removed, harmony and perfection will be restored.

The office of the one giving a treatment is to neutralize the erring belief through his substitution of the Truth. When the Subjective denial of perfection has been destroyed, the Divine Idea or Reality will appear.

Treatment has been defined as the induction of thought on the subjective side of life which sets the law in motion. The one giving the treatment recognizes each person as an individualized center of God-conscious Life, identified in Mind by the name he bears. The Universal Mind knows that there is a Robert Russell, because he, being self-conscious, knows that there is a Robert Russell. The Universal Mind, however, only knows Robert Russell by what Robert Russell knows about himself. What Robert Russell knows, the Universal Subjective Mind accepts and acts upon. It accepts him at his own estimate of himself and materializes this concept in his experience.

Mind gives back to you in the form of conditions what you think into It. Every time you think about yourself or your business, you are giving yourself a treatment. If you think Right Thought, you produce perfection; if you think wrong thought you produce imperfection. Conditions are always matched by the character of your thought; the point of contact in a treatment is the consciousness. If you are dissatisfied with conditions as they are, you must create the right concept. When the Universal Subjective Mind through the persistency of your thought has accepted the new concept as true, the demonstration takes place.

Jesus referred to the carnal mind when He said, The Prince of this world cometh and findeth nothing in me, that is, there was nothing in the current of His thought to oppose or neutralize Right Thought. Our realization must be just as clear.

We are saved by virtue of what we are in thought. Assume that you are the thing which you desire. Include yourself in the Universal Substance of God, and in this inner movement of consciousness, let your prayer be one of glorious realization that you are united with the perfect whole. Say —

MY LIFE IS PART OF HIS LIFE AS MY FINGER IS PART OF MY HAND. BECAUSE OF MY ONENESS WITH HIM, HIS LOVE IS EVER EXPRESSING ITSELF IN MY MIND AND SPIRIT, KEEPING ME IN PERFECT MENTAL POISE. HIS HEALTH IS EVER EXPRESSING ITSELF IN MY BODY, MAKING ME PERFECTLY WELL AND WHOLE. HIS ABUNDANCE IS EVER EXPRESSING ITSELF IN ME SO THAT I HAVE ALL THAT I CAN WISELY USE. AND HE WORKS IN ME EXCEEDING ABUNDANTLY ABOVE ALL THAT I CAN ASK OR THINK.

Keep in mind when praying for (treating) yourself or someone else that the work is done in the Universal Subjective Mind. As you know the Truth, you set the Law in motion. What is known in one part of Divine Mind is known in all parts. Your word (Right Thought) spoken for another will operate through that person no matter where he may be. No one can be absent from the Universal Subjective Mind.

Suppose that a Mr. X. comes to you for a treatment. He does not know that all is Mind, all is God, all is Universal Energy. He does not know that the physical appearance of sickness is in his consciousness. You sit down with him in the Silence; when you feel that he is perfectly still and receptive, you call his name in Mind and silently, "Mr. X., this Word is for you." Mr. X. is in that Mind and you are in that Mind. You know the Truth for him right where you are. Mr. X. must have a consciousness of health; until he has this consciousness, he will not be healed.

You contemplate the Perfect Man within your own consciousness; as you embody the Idea, you produce a perfect healing.

The consciousness of Mr. X. must change to the consciousness of his Perfection; the healing will take just as long as it takes for the subjective side of Mr. X.'s thought to accept the new concept as true.

Suppose that Mr. X. lives in Portland, Oregon and you live in New York City. He has written to you and asked for treatment. You begin by saying, "I am treating Mr. X. of Portland, Oregon," and then speak to Mr. X. directly. There is a definite reciprocal action and constant communion between all individual subjective minds; there is no separation in Spirit. You proceed in the consciousness that Mr. X. and you are both in the Universal Subjective Mind.

Use any Truth statement, knowing that the mind of the patient receives and acts upon it. Now say, "Mr. X., you are a perfect and complete manifestation of pure Spirit, and pure Spirit cannot be diseased; consequently, you are not diseased." This is the conclusion you must induce in the mind of Mr. X. You have set the Law in motion for him, but he must accept It. When his consciousness becomes convinced of Perfection, he will be healed.

The healing of a child is commensurate with the deep and absolute conviction of the one treating. Children are particularly responsive to our thought.

The business of the practitioner is to change the attitude of the patient, to reverse his mental polarity. You show him that the conditions from which he is suffering are the result of the habitual mental concepts he has held.

This outline is necessarily brief, but any treatment may be given in the same way. The Principle is identical in every need.

The method of the Silence is fundamentally for the purpose of bringing the patient into an understanding relationship with God; to bring his mind into reciprocal action with Divine Mind.

The patient who can consciously cooperate should say something like this as he is about to enter the Silence, "Into the care and keeping of God I give myself, all my ideas, all the affairs of my life and all the people about whom I am concerned or who are concerned about me. I rest from my labors, that I may do the works of Him that sent me."

In my book Victory Over Fear and Worry there are several suggestion for specific treatments.

The localizing of need for treatment and the factor of time are man-made. Perfect realization of Wholeness results instantaneous healing. Now is the accepted time… Now are we the sons of God… The hour cometh and now is.

Robert A. Russell

Appendix
Suggested Exercises to Produce Relaxation

Be silent all flesh before Jehovah. The physical body and the personal mind impinge upon each other; what affects one affects the other. Both must be eased from strain and effort.

There are two postures in which the Silence may be approached. In the horizontal position, the student lies flat upon his back on the bed, or preferably on the floor. I say on the floor because the muscles are compelled to relax in order to accommodate themselves to the hard surface and be comfortable. The body should rest as easily as possible, with no support under the head, and with the ankle bones about two inches apart. The position of the arms should be horizontal from the body, with the palms up and the fingers bent slightly inward.

The second suggested position is better for the beginner as this first position creates pressure upon the areas of the body where the vital energy is circulated in greatest volume. Often even advanced students do not get as good results in this first position as they do in the second.

The second position is the sitting posture. This is the method which most of the Masters use; it consists of sitting upon a stool or bench of sufficient height to allow the feet to rest flat upon the floor. If one chooses the sitting posture, he must sit comfortably with the head, neck and chest in a perfectly vertical line and the hands, with the palms up and the fingers slightly curved, resting loosely upon the thighs. The trunk of the body should rest upon the ribs and not on the spinal column.

In both positions, the subject should breathe deeply but gently. Natural and correct breathing will make the body resilient and will eliminate much poison through oxidation. One exhalation often contains sufficient poison to vitiate a barrel of air. When the breathing exercises are faithfully performed, they will remove depression and lassitude from the mind and body, but their chief function is to make the mind and body insensible to the distractions of the physical world.

There is a divine Substance in breath akin to food, and taking your exercise before breakfast will oft times serve as a full meal. You can live for days without food but can live briefly without breathing. Breath is the life of God. It was not until God breathed into man the Breath of Life that he became a living soul.

In the Bible, we have unmistakable evidence and records of the bestowal of gifts and blessings through the process of breathing on people. One of these is recorded in the life of St. Paul. Coveting for a particular group of people the Truth of the Spirit of God, he breathed on them and said, Receive ye the Holy Ghost.

The spiritual breath which I am recommending for your use in the Silence is not the atmospheric breath but that rarefied substance known as ether. This is the Omnipresent Breath of God and the Life that penetrates all matter. Few people know very much about this etheric breath, and most of what is known comes from the far East. But we do know that ether penetrates all substance, and that by the act of faith, it can be transmuted into energy, life and health. Think of it as the Water of Life, cleaning the soul and body.

Seated in the position for the Silence, breathe deeply five or six times in rapid succession and come to a complete pause.

Then inhale slowly and evenly through both nostrils, while mentally counting seven; then hold the breath during seven counts and exhale slowly and evenly at the same time mentally counting seven more. Repeat seven times with a minute's pause between each breath.

The holding process will require an exercise of the will. After the intake, the breath should be held in the lungs, not in the throat. A special effort should be made to expand the chest muscles and to press the diaphragm down without lifting the shoulders. The air should be pushed down as far as possible and the throat muscles relaxed.

The object of this exercise is depth of breathing and the idea is to press the air as far down as possible before pressing it up into the lungs. When the chest is expanded and the lungs feel tight, exhale the air naturally through the mouth but keep it under control while counting seven.

The next exercise is somewhat more difficult but equally important. Repeat the exercise above and when both the lower region and upper region are filled to capacity, take in more air through the mouth to the point where there is a feeling of discomfort. Exhale as you did before. The secret of effective breathing is to breathe naturally through both nostrils at the same time. If the practice seems difficult at first, do not crowd yourself. Use two repetitions the first week and increase them until you reach the maximum of seven. When you are able to enter the Silence readily, it will not be necessary to use seven repetitions, but it is advisable always to use at least one.

When taking a fresh supply of breath into the body, hold some such thought as this:

THE BREATH OF GOD IS MY LIFE. THE BREATH OF GOD IS OMNIPRESENT. IT NOW WASHES MY BODY CLEAN. I INHALE THIS BREATH AND I AM QUICKENED, RENEWED, VITALIZED AND STRENGTHENED. IN THIS SPIRITUAL BREATH WHICH NOW SURGES THROUGH EVERY FIBER AND ATOM OF MY BEING, I AM YOUNG, WHOLE AND FREE.

If the breathing exercises have been performed properly, there will be a warmth and a tingling sensation all through the body. You are now ready for relaxation.

As the mind relaxes, the body will relax, and the reverse is equally true. I AM cannot take possession of the body and fill it with new life and energy while there is any tension or contraction in any part of it.

As we learn to use the Principle, we shall be able to control the body of the physical world. We shall learn how to bring it under the subjection and dominion of the Spirit.

The consciousness which envelops and pervades the body is the intelligent principle of the I AM. This intelligence resides in every electron, ion, atom and molecule, and responds to the commands of our own Divine Mind. Each one obeys the imperious demands of the Spirit within. We train the body to relax through the spoken word, to become a clean and supple instrument for the Spirit.

PHYSICAL EXPERIMENT No. 1

Sit perfectly still for seven minutes without moving a nerve or muscle; then raise the arm and mentally draw the blood out of it into some other part of the body until it feels absolutely lifeless. If, when you drop it to the side again, it has no feeling, it is relaxed. The same thing can be done with the legs and feet.

PHYSICAL EXPERIMENT No. 2

Hold one of your hands in front of you with the fingers as far apart as possible, and keep each finger from trembling for a period of five minutes.

The most luxurious feeling which can come over one is to be perfectly relaxed. The command, Let this mind be in you which was also in Christ Jesus, implies relaxation. As we harmonize our minds with the Universal Mind, we relax mentally. When the mind is relaxed, the body, which is its effect, will also become relaxed.

Now squeeze every part of the body through contracting it as tightly as you can, just as you would squeeze a sponge in a bucket of water to make it absorbent. Do this three times. There must be no tension in your effort to relax. Feel the very pulse and presence of the Spirit as you relax. Center the whole attention in whatever part of the body you are working with but withdraw consciousness from that particular part after you leave it.

The chief idea in relaxation is to become absolutely unconscious of the body. Consciousness will always follow where your attention leads it. Address every part of the body as one having authority. After intensive contraction of the body, center the attention at the top of the head.

Certain important sets of nerves and muscles are found both inside and outside of the cranium. We think of this part of the body as the point of distribution of the vital energy and the area which must be relaxed first.

Through an act of mind, hold the whole consciousness at that place. Then visualize a white Light as enveloping and penetrating every part of the body. I am the light of the world. Mentally picture this Light as enveloping the brain and radiating from the neck and the spine with a tremendous and almost binding glow. This white Light is symbolical of the purity and healing power of the Christ consciousness. It is the Light of the fourth-dimensional Spiritual consciousness which blinded St. Paul on the highway to Damascus, which illuminated the face of Moses as he descended from Mount Sinai, which enveloped Jesus as He descended from the Mount of Transfiguration. White light is a cooling light with a very rapid and high vibration. It is part of the glory which you had with God before the world was.

With this white Light diffusing the entire body, say to the muscles in the head:

Be still and know that I am God. Be still and know that I am God. Be still and know that I am God.

Then feel the Inner Presence (Spirit) operating in this part. Firmly but gently bid these nerves and muscles to let go of all tension by repeating with deep feeling the following words:

Peace, Peace, Peace, Peace, Peace, be still.

Relax, Relax, Relax, Relax.

Now bring the consciousness to the nerves and muscles in the forehead and repeat the same process; at the same time, feel the flesh and wrinkles smoothing out under the power of your word. The head symbolizes the capacity to know God.

Next bring the attention and consciousness into the eyes. Before using the formula for relaxation, squeeze the eyeballs as tightly as possible with the eyelids; then lift the eyeballs up as far as possible; then turn them to each side and then down as far as possible. Rest; then repeat the formula and let go of all eye tension. The eyes are the capacity of spiritual discernment.

The face is the next area to be relaxed, and in this connection we think of the ears, the nose, the mouth, teeth, tongue, palate and taste (the gustatory nerves) and of the spiritual qualities which correspond to each.

The ear is the capacity to understand.
The nose is the capacity for pursuing a train of thought.
The mouth is the capacity to rejoice, praise and respond.
The teeth are the capacity of analyzing and dissecting ideas.
The tongue is the capacity of enjoyment.

The palate and taste are the capacity to appreciate God's ideas.

Then relax the shoulders and hands. The shoulders are symbolical of the capacity to carry burdens. Come unto me, all ye that labor and are heavy laden... Take my yoke upon you, and learn of me... For my yoke is easy, and my burden is light. When the shoulders are relaxed, you should feel a general letdown through the upper part of the body. The personal mind should drop all its sense of burden.

The arms are symbolical of God's power to lift loads; the hands are the ability to grasp God's ideas. When the arms and hands are perfectly relaxed, they will be so limp that there is no feeling in them.

Now turn your attention to the trunk of the body, which contains most of the vital organs. This is the house of the lungs, the heart, the liver, the stomach, the kidneys, the solar plexus (sympathetic nervous system) and the abdomen.

The solar plexus occupies the most central position in the body. It contains the largest group of ganglia in the whole system. It is the abdominal brain which receives and distributes nerves impulses and currents to all the abdominal brain which receives and distributes nerve impulses and currents to all the abdominal organs, supplying the main organs of nutrition and assimilation with nervous energy. It is the seat of the emotions, referred to many times in the Bible as the heart. The sympathetic nervous system is subjective in nature, controlling the involuntary processes of the body, the rhythmical beating of the heart, contraction and dilation of the arteries, the peristaltic action of the gastro-intestinal tract, and the secretions of the various glands. The solar plexus may be said to be the most important region of the body, and often while relaxing this brain, people are instantly healed.

In relaxing each organ in succession, use the following formula:

Be still and know that I am harmony. Relax, Relax, Relax, Relax, Relax.

Leaving the trunk, turn your attention to the lower limbs, the hips, the thighs, the legs, the feet and the toes. For this part of the body, use the words, Peace, be still.

When every part of the body is relaxed, pause on the threshhold of the Silence and say something like this:

I HAVE NOW REMOVED FROM MY CONSCIOUSNESS ALL SENSE OF MATERIAL THINGS AND MY FLESH IS SILENT BEFORE GOD. MY MIND AND MY BODY ARE AT REST IN HIM. I AM OVERSHADOWED BY HIS PROTECTING POWER. ALL TENSENESS IS RELAXED; ALL WEARINESS IS RESTED. EACH NERVE, EACH MUSCLE AND EACH ORGAN OF MY BODY IS RECEPTIVE TO TRUTH. THE SPIRIT OF LIFE FLOWS THROUGH ME LIKE A PEACEFUL RIVER. DIVINE HARMONY NOW MANIFESTS IN ME AS PERFECT BEING AND I FUNCTION IN DIVINE ORDER.

Instead of the breathing exercises already given, you may draw in twenty-one regular and rhythmic breaths, and then hold your breath. Listen to your heart. At first the pulsations will come faster; then they will become slow and strong. Your whole being will then be enveloped by a great sense of peace; a feeling of tranquility and assurance will come to you. It may be you will see light flashing before your eyes, or hear strange sounds, such as bells ringing or the friction of wheels. These are not psychic phenomena; do not be disturbed.

Consciously think of your breathing; say to yourself with each inhalation, "With every breath I draw, I am breathing in the very Breath of God"; and with each exhalation say, "With this expiration, the strain, fears, limitations, worries and poisons of my life are being expelled."

After you have held your breath as long as you can without strain or discomfort, then repeat the process of twenty-one regular and rhythmic breaths three times, and you will find that you possess a deep sense of peace such as you never had before. You are then ready to proceed to the other steps in the mastery of the Silence.

The breathing exercises should be taken only by people who are in sound health and who are possessed of strong hearts.

FINI

Note on Robert A Russell: RobertARussell.Org

I have spent the last 5 years tracking down the works of this exceptional mystic and I believe I have found approximately 95% of his lost works. I am constantly on the search for his lost titles, here is a list of our current titles:

GOD Works Through Faith
GOD Works Through You
GOD Works Through Silence
All Things Made New
Dry Those Tears
I have Found the Way
Getting Better Results from Spiritual Practice
In Spite of Everything
Making the Contact
Quickest Way to Everything Good
Talk yourself Out of It
Talk Yourself INTO it
The Laboratory of Silence
This Works
Victory over fear and Worry
Vital Points in Demonstration
You Can Get What You Want
You Too Can Be Prosperous
You Try It
The Answer Will Come

If you are currently living in Colorado, or have a family member or know anyone that has anymore of his works and want to help us continue his spiritual legacy, please drop us an email to aepublish@gmail.com

We would be happy to purchase your books.
Thank You, Barry Peterson, Publisher